This
is the

FUTURE DIARY

Of

_____

FUTURE DIARY

BY

MARK VICTOR HANSEN

PATTY
HANSEN,
KEITH TERRY,
AND
CAROL FOREMAN BROCKFIELD
EDITORS

MARK VICTOR HANSEN
PUBLISHING
COMPANY
NEWPORT BEACH, CALIFORNIA 92660

Photographed by
Jaren Dahlstrom, John Pearson,
Richard Stacks, Susan Katz
and Terrence Toole

Designed by Paul Hobson, San Francisco
First Printing
C 1980 Showcase Publishing Company
Second Printing
C 1983 Mark Victor Hansen Publishing Company
Third Printing
C 1985 Mark Victor Hansen Publishing Company
Fourth Printing
C 1986 Mark Victor Hansen Publishing Company
Fifth Printing
C 1989 Mark Victor Hansen Publishing Company

Mark Victor Hansen
Publishing Company
P.O. Box 7665
Newport Beach, California 92660

Library of Congress Catalog No. 80-51759

ISBN: 0-912965-00-2

Printed in the
United States of Amcrica

DEDICATION

This is dedicated to my beautiful Patty, who is my best friend, greatest supporter, and the most wonderful wife that I know.

I am thankful that I created her in my original **Future Diary**, and now she is mine.

TABLE

OF

CONTENTS

INTRODUCTION.........................9
BENEFITS OF YOUR FUTURE DIARY.....16
FUTURE DIARY 20
YOUR TREMENDOUS VICTORIOUS
AUTOBIOGRAPHY 27
ESTABLISH YOUR PLAN 33
CRAZY GOALS 43
GOAL PREPARATION 48
THE LAW OF ASSUMPTION 53
EVALUATE YOUR GOALS 63
AWAKEN A HIDDEN GENIUS 92
MIND SOLUTION 101
GOAL SETTING IS FREE...............102
SUPPLY IS INFINITE 106
MONEY 114
BIG GOALS 119
POWERFULLY FOCUSED 127
IMAGINARY CONVERSATIONS 133
SELF-PORTRAIT 135
THE DREAM GOALS GAME 137
FIVE MORE TECHNIQUES 139
NOW IT'S UP TO YOU 143

Dedicate yourself
to the good you deserve
and desire for yourself.
Give yourself peace of mind.
You deserve to be happy.

INTRODUCTION

Goal-setting is fun, rewarding, and result-getting. Once you have experienced its benefits and fulfillments, you will become a regular, ritualistic and systematic goal-setter and goal-getter. It underwrites your being, doing, and having options in life. A goal, the dictionary says, is "an aim or purpose." Life means more with goals than without goals.

Life's *being* options include being happy; being healthy; being loving, loved, and beloved; being successful; being prosperous, rich, and abundant; being wise, witty, and wonderful; being intelligent; being strong and self-confident; being enthusiastic, enlightened, enriched, edified, and entertained. Throughout life you can win prizes, recognition, stature and gain accomplishments for yourself and others; at your best you can hit home runs for all of humanity, just as did Disney, Einstein, Edison, Carver and Fuller. You deserve a splendid home, terrific relationships, peace of mind, full self-expression, and the total joy of living. Life is to be experienced and expressed, fully and joyously. As Helen Keller said, "Life is either a daring adventure, or nothing."

Pre-determine the objectives you want to accomplish. Think big, act big, and set out to accomplish big results. Big goals turn on the energy in your eighteen billion brain cells. Your vast mind power is waiting for you to get turned on and stay turned on. Those bountiful,

9

beautiful, totally available and probably under-used brain cells want you to be committed to zesty, dynamic, and exciting accomplishments. No one has ever used 100 percent of their ability. Invest yours toward what you want, to the exclusion of what you don't want. Your abilities multiplied by your motivation equals your performance. Goal-setting stimulates and invigorates your motivation. That is why one needs *too many goals* to stay rip-roaringly charged up and enthused.

Andrew Carnegie started in business as a day laborer earning 28 cents a day. He had written a goal — to spend the first half of his life earning a fortune and the second half giving it away. He ultimately gave over 465 million dollars to the American Library System.

Goals work. They empower you to do more for yourself, others and, in fact, all of humanity. We are just now gaining the perspective of having five billion humans on spaceship earth. We are, for the first time in history, acknowledging that our planet is truly small and shrinking, theoretically, as communication increases. Information and people are really in motion worldwide, and we feel what others are doing. In business, media, entertainment, education, transportation, and so forth, the new model starts with world and comes back to our country, state (province), city, and then us. That is why we must set gigantic goals. We are the first generation in history to have the proper tools and the awareness to use them.

When we were children, most of us day-dreamed and imagined untold wonders in our futures. The problems? No one taught us the almost magic principle of writing down our own future good. Too many people grow up and leave their dreams and enthusiasm for really living behind in childhood. Re-awaken yourself and use this phenomenal tool to re-excite yourself to your own greatness, confident living and full self-expression. It will help you to re-think your life's goals and to stimulate a never-ending dynamic development process of self-learning. Let this be the first of literally hundreds of **Future Diaries** that you autobiographically script to take you to places, people, situations, and circumstances that no one else has ever previously created or could have created. Be yourself and maximize yourself positively and correctly in all areas of your life. If you will just write in your **Future Diary** all your desired future good, you will have a bigger role in front of you than everything you have done in the past. Become a part of the new breed of growth-oriented giants and superstar achievers who actively and repetitively use the deceptively simple creative process of writing down personal goals.

I have applied the process and have accomplished great things. Many people reading my resume say that someone my age could not have done all I've done. I believe in what Elsa Maxwell said, "Intolerance of mediocrity has been the main prop of my independence." I really have done all that I say and even more, because I am aware of my orientation and desires. They are written down. I am forever taking appropriate action, and goals and forever being realized. Once one gets into the swing of it, it becomes effortless. I know now, by experience, that when I write a goal, I will accomplish it. It is inevitable, if not immediate.

Let me give one recent example. When in 1974 I started professional speaking, I recorded that one day I wanted my own television show. I knew that production costs started at ten thousand dollars per half-hour show. I wanted a normal session's run of twenty-six one-half hour shows. I wrote it down. I knew the subconscious mind always figures out how to get anything one really wants if one wants to get it long enough.

It took nine years, but so what? One lives (spiritually) forever. In 1983 I was invited by a local cable television company to do the Mark Victor Hansen Show, from Newport Beach, California. When invited, I politely said, "Thank you, I've been expecting your call." It got a surprised reception.

"Why?" the program director inquired.

"Because I wrote down that I would have my own show which I would help write, edit, and direct, and that I would own the copyright, too, even though someone else would invest in the show. You're it. Thank you. I've been readying myself for you." Everything I wrote down came true exactly as I had visualized and even more. The studio crew and I became great friends; we all worked zealously to create a dynamite finished product that was a blessing to all who viewed it.

Please note that when I wrote down my goal, I had no money. Therefore, I was undercapitalized, I was an embryonic speaker with big visions and burning desire. At the time cable television did not even exist as we know it today. For me, my imagination created cable television so that my dream could be fulfilled. Dream great dreams and write them down for future accomplishment. The process of doing so is virtually free — all you need is paper and pen. Remember that your imagination and visualization processes create your future reality. What you haven't been or haven't done until now does not matter at all. What you envision doing matters exclusively. Write down your goal, do it, and then you too can say, "I've done it, but I've only just begun."

When you write down *too many goals*, your mind will prioritize them for you and work automatically to awaken new ways to accomplish more in less time. Within months you will feel new peace of mind, accompanied by a sense of direction and relative simplicity. The technique of writing down your goals is old, but tragically and unforgivably under used. All of us, one at a time, need to be repetitively sold on this technique — not told this technique — until it becomes as natural and automatic as breathing out and breathing in. Using this technique will make you a powerful person and a force for good in the universe. You will become a leader in world productivity and social change, and a promoter of a quality lifestyle for all — everywhere.

Once you are moving, get totally committed to your tasks. Move forward confidently, picturing exclusively in your mind's eye the results you want to the exclusion of what you don't want. Remember this statement by Mother Theresa: "To keep a lamp burning we have to keep putting oil in it."

Keep a pen in hand as you read on, for this is your personal **Future Diary**. In it you will find pages with room to define yourself, define your goals and desires, and begin to script your own future. Write in it, expand it and overflow its pages with everything you want to be, do, or have. Dream, fantasize, and expect your ideas to come into being.

With the **Future Diary** as your tool you can become the world's most important conceiver — if you will. Please do and write to tell me about your results.

Mark Victor Hansen

Newport Beach, California

January, 1989

When you know clearly
what you want
you'll wake up every morning
excited about life.

CHAPTER 1

BENEFITS OF YOUR FUTURE DIARY

The following are the benefits of writing in your new diary. It will:

— stimulate your creative thinking.

— introduce you to your inner thoughts, feelings, moods, attitudes, and beliefs.

— clarify your relationships (family, friends, and career).

— give you peace of mind.

— assist you in making decisions — large and small.

— help you learn more and learn faster.

— be your private place.

— be a special place to put pictures, quotes, clippings, personal comments, interviews, and ideas.

— help you thoroughly create your life's agenda.

— be a treasure map of your heart's desires.

— acquaint you with your inner advisor.

— invoke your own personal wisdom and strength.

— be a tool for personal growth.

— provide a place to write for pleasure and self-guidance.

— create your own unique autobiography, and make it a great one.

— help you discover new solutions to problems.

— effectively process your life experience.

— help you write with spontaneity, honesty, depth, clarity, humor, and feeling.

— help you recognize your profound subconscious.

— allow you to become self-responsible
  and more self-actualizing.

— develop fabulous friends.

— develop deeper love.

— have financial freedom.

— encourage you.

— be a source of play.

— be a healthful release of tension,
  anxiety, and unexpressed feelings.

— build a personal sense of wholeness
  and coherence.

— allow you to experience the full range
  of your imagination.

— develop a habit of writing your own experience — past, present, and future.

— allow you to hear your inner voice of
  intuition.

— be a place to collect material for many
  creative uses.

— advise yourself.

- clarify your goal-setting and getting.

- nourish yourself with friendship.

- increase self-acceptance, self-esteem, self-reliance, and self-worth.

- be a path to self-awareness and self-knowledge.

- rehearse your future behavior.

- provide a technique to focus effort and energy.

- be a memory aid.

- be an organizer and prioritizer establisher.

- be a way to profit from and enjoy solitude.

- help you develop the skill of self-expression.

- be a place to relax and refresh yourself.

CHAPTER 2

FUTURE DIARY

Future Diary is a tool that will change your life from good to phenomenally good. Write down *all* of your goals, hopes, dreams, high aspirations, and high ideals, and then take action towards them. As you progressively accomplish the desires of your heart, write the word *victory* next to your accelerating achievements. As you intuitively and practically know, goal-setting is goal-getting. It is a recent discovery that goal achievement makes you feel good because goal-getting stimulates endorphins to rush through your body which causes a natural high, according to psychiatrist Dr. William Glasser, The Reality Therapist.

Goals are magnets that pull you toward them. As they are accomplished, go on to higher and higher goals. Constantly keep writing more goals, and you will experience and enjoy a great, grand, and terrific life.

All success philosophers suggest that you need one major goal in life. That is incomplete. My heart-felt recommendation is that you need *too many goals*, not too few. As Mae West said, "too much of a good thing is wonderful!"

There are three great reasons to have too many goals:

1. Different goals have different gestation rates, i.e., a chicken egg takes twenty-one days to break into life, a human embryo takes nine months, and an elephant takes two years. Goals are processed into reality based on your real inner desires. Some goals are inherently easy to achieve. As you become a masterful goal-setter, you will be amazed and intrigued with the speed of achievement.

2. When one goal is completed, it loses its power and importance. Think about the last new car you really wanted. Once you got it and used it, it became quality transportation. You then needed a new goal.

3. The world is abundant. There is no lack in the universe. You can have almost everything you really want. Use your creative imagination! As you do, consider that Walt Disney was one man who possessed, like you do, an imagination and the ability to write down his dreams and then go for them. His objectives were so thorough that he spent fifteen years planning Disneyland. He built it in one year and had twelve million visitors during the first year. Disney was a self-actualizing person who enjoyed full self-expression through the process of goal-setting and goal-getting. When Disneyland was complete, he said, "This isn't good enough, I can do better," and started on Disney World in Orlando, Florida. Goal-setting

for Disney, for you, and for me is an ecstatic journey. It is not a destination.

Future Diary is your dynamic, expanding, and evolving autobiography in process. Life is not an end result but rather an enjoyable, never-ending sequence of meaningful, almost momentary destinations. Disney's dreams were so well scripted and modeled that, posthumously, we are still realizing what he imagined. In October of 1982, his greatest dream, EPCOT City (Experimental Prototypical Community of Tomorrow) opened seventeen years after his death. You can do the same and more. Start writing lots and lots of goals.

One lady asked me, "Mark, what's your biggest goal?" My answer was, "to motivate total humanity to its own success." During my million-plus hours of life, with the aid of all media, I would like to expose every living human to the consciousness that they can dream great dreams and build foundations under them. The tools exist in this book. You can help me by sharing this book with everyone you know, I believe the concept is as elementary as teaching a man or woman to fish (set and get goals) and he or she is fed for life.

Everyone has an intrinsic right to love, food, health, and shelter. You can be an effective expander of this consciousness by self-setting and getting goals.

Incidentally, I telepathically caught your thought that communicating to upwards of five billion humans is impossible. In days gone by many concepts we take for granted today (televisions, telephones, phonographs, electricity, airplanes) were deemed impossible. Let's say I don't reach everyone. That's okay. I got to you, and you may be the one to reach everyone. The job is worthy, no matter who accomplishes it. Roger Bannister proved that the four-minute mile was possible. Now it is commonplace. (Over five hundred individuals have run the four-minute mile, and now the winner of the Boston Marathon averages a four-minute forty-seven second mile.) This is because we've broken through the mental barrier. There's a mental barrier currently to believing everyone's interested and attentive to the consciousness of goals. I like being driven by big goals, and this dream, like all others, starts general and becomes specific through repetitious review and more ideation.

My dream for the end of my long life will be that I have not yet achieved all of my goals. I hope the same is true of you.

My question to you is, "What's your biggest goal?" Have you expanded it again and again? Let me give examples of individuals who have set, reset, and forever expanded their goals. My hope is that you will read the biographies and autobiographies of these and other greats and be inspired to totally outperform yourself. A partial list includes the following: Dr. Thomas Alva Edison, Edward Land, Dr. R. Buckminster Fuller, Dr. Armand Hammer, Liberace, William Randolph Hearst, Kitty O'Neill, Rich DeVos, Mary Kay, Clement Stone, Zig Ziglar, and Dr. George Washington Carver.

Show me a thoroughly satisfied man
and I will show you a failure.

Thomas Alva Edison (1847 - 1931)

I WANT

Write Down Every Good Thing You Want to Be, Do, or Have.

CHAPTER 3

YOUR TREMENDOUS

VICTORIOUS

AUTOBIOGRAPHY

The average human alive today will live in excess of 500,000 hours. Longevity specialists like Dirk Pearson suggest that if you were accident proof, there is no physiological or biological reason you could not live to be eight hundred years old. Medicine and science have extended the life-span and will continue to make enormous, almost unbelievable and inconceivable advances in the near future. Your life hours are inevitably going to increase as you decide to think right, eat right, sleep right, exercise right, and maintain right habits by writing down what's right for you to do. Let's say by doing all this you double your available life experience to over one million hours. My wife and I have made that choice and are constantly affirming it and options for renewal and expansion of our lives together.

Given all those hours, you can spend your time as most of humanity does — getting little return for your investment in this life. Most people are too busy making a living to really live vitally, fully, and dynamically. The truth is that they've never thought out what you are reading now. Furthermore, they have never bothered to script their own life agenda and become personally decisive. I want to excite you to get your own personal directional compass and invest your million life hours exclusively toward accomplishing what you want. It will take discipline. I agree with Katherine Hepburn, who said that "Without discipline, there's no life at all."

Recognize, as every thoughtful person does, that the ultimate, soul-satisfying, yet powerful wisdom is *Love is for the sake of loving . . . to serve for the sake of serving . . . . to give for the sake of giving.* As you do this, the law of exchange states that for each outward act there is a multiplying equal and opposite inward act. This law has many similar names, such as "the law of compensation." As you sow (in consciousness) so you will reap (in experience); give and you shall receive. It's all true. Just do it.

As you do, new intuitions, inspirations, ideas, thought-forms, and hunches will gush into your mind. They come as you self-interrogate yourself with questions of desire. Be sure to record all these vital, viable insights immediately into your **Future Diary**. Often the angel of inspiration will visit you in the middle of the night, during the tantalizing relevant state of consciousness just prior to sleep or upon arising. Be ever ready with paper and pen to jot down and capture your own great ideas. Otherwise they could be lost forever.

Catalog your ideas. Review them regularly, and new insights will forever flood your mind, as happened to

Thomas Edison, Bill Lear, and Buckminster Fuller. There is only one mind, and that infinite intelligence of God is as available to you as to any other person. You need only know it exists. Trust it, commune with it, tap it, and use your revelations.

You will soon discover that you were de-geniused sometime after birth by negative thinking, belief systems, and life assumptions of peers, parents, and teachers. They meant well, but were probably ignorant of the genius power inside each of us.

Regular, systematic autobiographical **Future Diary** work — as Socrates said, "Know thyself" — will teach you how much mind power you really have. You can do, be, and have almost anything. You will learn the science of yourself.

The more you do it, the better you get at phenomenal result-getting in all dimensions of your life. I have purposely repeated that I want you to have *too many goals*, not too few.

My own **Future Diary** has in excess of 398 pages of goals. As I accomplish one, I write down *victory* in the left-hand margin in bold, bright colors. This inspires me to go for bigger, bolder, and more far-reaching horizons. It repetitiously reminds me that "I am somebody special, and I can do it." I encourage you to similarly encourage yourself. Even affirm, "I am a self-encourager." You need to be to become super-successful. If you don't positively and correctly appreciate yourself, no one else will either.

Aggregating **Future Diary** victory statements will help you grow to be all you can be. The law of life is the law of growth; if you choose not to grow, you begin to die. **Future Diary** is your tool to grow onward, upward, and Godward.

The success of mankind
begins with the individual.
If you understand these principles
of personal achievement,
who knows what
humanity can achieve.

WRITE DOWN YOUR DREAMS

I want to operate a successful business
I want to grow spiritually every day of my life
I want to live in a house by the ocean
I want to love and be loved

CHAPTER 4

ESTABLISH YOUR PLAN

The mechanics of goal-setting are simple. Just write down your every good desire in all areas of your experience. This is the best way to grow strong and to ensure that you lead a rich, meaningful life filled to overflowing with joy, love, success, health, happiness, prosperity, higher spiritual states of mind and money.

Most individuals have no idea how easy goal-setting really is. It works the same as writing a weekly grocery list. With that list in your hand you generally obtain everything on the list and then some extra items for good measure. Without a list, often we neglect to obtain a critically important item and have to wastefully spend time going back to re-do what could have been done in one simple visit. Similarly, super-achievers always transcend their stated goals simply because they have positive momentum, definiteness of purpose, and their directional compass knows its short and long-term orientation. Alfred Lord Whitehead said, "Great dreamer's dreams are never fulfilled, they are always transcended."

At Yale University in 1953, the graduating class was polled to see how many had written goals that were definite, positive, specific, believable, desirable, and attainable. Only three percent had such goals. Twenty years later this chronofile/longevity study was reopened, only to discover that the students with written goals had accomplished sum totally more than the other 97 percent of the class combined. The message is clear: Become a "three percenter" and set goals. It's likely that by doing so you will become a super-achiever, big-time winner, and make a positive difference in life. Write down your goals and keep adding more and more and more. Please help expand this percentage by doing it regularly, systematically, and purposefully. I am being purposefully redundant when I say, "Have too many goals."

As I stated before, my personal **Future Diary** has in excess of 398 pages of written goals. I am forever adding more. My mind, like yours, is a teleological mechanism that proceeds to figure how to do anything I want to do. If you know that you want something, the how will manifest itself.

Learning life's most vital process of goal establishment will help you to do what you want to do, be what you want to be, have what you want to have, because you will learn to think what you want to think. You will literally experience life transforming experience after life transforming experience. It requires work, the hardest kind of work that there is — *thinking* — your thinking, choicing, and re-choicing for that which you will be rejoicing. Think thoroughly through life's most important questions: "What do I really want?" Because whatever you want, wants you more than you want it!

You can learn to be a master goal-getter in fifteen minutes a day. Merely establish a fifteen-minute daily time for study, planning, and goal-setting. Early in the morning when your mind is fresh and clear or late at night just prior to sleep is preferable. Simply bring out your **Future Diary** with pen in hand and lovingly review your desires and goals. Practice it long enough to become automatic in setting and getting goals. Expect to have a fresh crop of new ideas telling you how to achieve your already set goals and add new ones.

Always have a pen in hand so that you can add thought flashes that will gush forth. At the end of one month of twice or more daily reviewing, writing, and treasure-mapping in your **Future Diary**, you will have accomplished the following: 1) You will be the author of your own life; 2) You will understand the life-creating principles, promises of a goal oriented balanced life and lifestyle; 3) You will have started thinking out what is truly important to you; 4) You will develop a lifetime habit that will provide you with countless benefits, undeclared dividends, and pluses in every area of your life's experience and expression; 5) You will discover that results are worth the effort of reading, studying, learning, and thinking about your **Future Diary**.

Through the years I have watched thousands of individuals, some bright, some average, with all ranges of academic and non-academic backgrounds. I have marveled at what wonderful things happened — in every case — when each individual developed the habit of daily feeding his mind with goals. I've watched ship-wrecked human lives transformed into lovable, capable, talent-using, talent-expanding individuals who became giants in their respective disciplines. It's exciting to watch failures renew

35

themselves and their lifestyles because they become committed to their goals. Goal-setting doesn't cost a cent; it's underwritten by activity that benefits everyone.

Write down your goals. When they are written down on paper and become inscribed on your mind, they will ultimately and inevitably show up in your future. Today's thoughts become tomorrow's reality.

When writing in your **Future Diary**, *write your easy ideas first*. Write fast; write everything from your feelings, body, mind, or whatever. It's a way to develop yourself by self-watching your goals develop over time. That's why you should date your every goal. Moving quickly will help you tap your vital, valuable inner resources. Allow yourself the freedom to do intuitive writing and drawing and be open to uncovering your inner destiny. This intense self-study will open you to an unexplored internal reality that will make your external day-to-day reality ever better. Experiment with your diary — do it differently at different times. Some individuals feel most inclined to start or end their day reading, reflecting, and writing in their dairy. Perhaps you want to do it at a special time, in a special place, or during your work week. That's your prerogative. My only request is that you create a system and then stick to it for over thirty days. Then it will be a habit forever.

J. C. Penney once said, "Give me a stock clerk with a goal, and I will give you a stock clerk who makes history."

It seems too good to be true. You can set goals, prioritize them, and realize them. What stifles, stops, and thwarts this great process is energy diffusing doubt and indecision. Your source of assurance that it's "do-able" is that so many others have done it; and if they can, you can.

Personally interview the ten most successful super-achievers available to you and ask them about their goal-setting habits. Seasoned experts have so indoctrinated themselves that their subtle processes are now effortless. This will boost your confidence in goal achievement.

Be immune to bad news. Daily reading of the newspaper will depress, deflate, anger, and annoy you. Generally, it is the sensationalistic worst expression that one-tenth of one percent of humanity is involved in. My recommendation is that prior to reading newspapers, news magazines, or watching or listening to the news, you simply say, "*I am immune to this.*" Instead of ingesting all the (bad) news fit to print and becoming repetitively upset at world circumstances and conditions, I encourage you to read your **Future Diary**. My friend, Cavett Robert, says, "Either you are a creature of circumstance or the creator of circumstance. You are either the cause or the result." Be the casual factor in your experience. Write it down, Now! If you repeat this self-motivator, "Write it down, now," fifty times a day for a month, you will believe it and achieve accordingly — extra-ordinarily. You can't arrive at a destination you haven't scheduled or return from a trip you didn't take. You can't achieve goals you haven't set.

To overcome your fear of goal-setting, just take action. Action cures all depression. Happy people are always active people. Action facilitates your ability to be fruitful and multiply. Doing this guarantees you will prosper and have good success.

You are never "too busy." You have all the time there is. Your spirit is immortal and will live forever. You refresh and renew your mind by reviewing your goals. Invest a little, give time daily in contemplation, meditation, study, planning, and growing with a pen in hand and your **Future Diary** ready to receive your every impress of thought. It will probably become the most important part of your day.

You eat regularly, why not have regular mental meals in your **Future Diary**? Discipline is the name of the game. Paul Anderson, whose daily weight-lifting made him the strongest man in the world; Terry Bradshaw, a premier football quarterback; Billie Jean King, who has won over nineteen tennis championships; or Arnold Schwartznegger, who has won all the important physical culturist titles, including "Mr. Universe"; Dr. Isaac Asimov, who has written and published over 239 books on science fiction and science fact, novels, and Bible commentaries — all have added discipline to their abundant talents. If you do likewise, you will become a superstar in your field.

When preparing to write in your **Future Diary**, take three relaxing deep breaths; then close your outer eyes and open the inner eye of your creative imagination and prepare yourself to write down your special accomplishments. Really plan to be outstanding at whatever you plan, whether it's business, play, family, lifestyle goals, or whatever. Inside of every human being is something special, just waiting to be recognized by writing it down and then released into beautiful splendor by taking the correct action. It's sort of like Michelangelo's *David*. He visualized it perfect and then released it from the rock with precise chipping.

Goals are a preview
of future events
and experiences
in your life.

I WANT PRECISELY

Attain your desires by picturing them keenly, clearly, crisply in your mind.

Write a detailed description of your major goals.

If you write
a big enough personal agenda
you will help
all of mankind.
Does the bumblebee know
the vast scope of its job
as it pollinates a flower?

CHAPTER 5

CRAZY GOALS

You owe it to yourself and humanity to set gigantic, seemingly impossible goals that will help everyone. Whether you have high aim or low aim, you will hit it; if you have low aim, you have no aim and will hit nothing. It grieves me to watch individuals squander their lives because they have neglected the process of writing down their personal goals. The process of setting and getting goals is fun.

Remember and remind yourself often that great goals attract great energy and mediocre goals attract little energy. Therefore, deciding in favor of luxuries will ultimately give you the luxuries and inadvertently pay the rent; whereas mere attempts to pay the rent will leave you with unpaid rent and no luxuries. Go for the big dreams with lots of excitement, personal growth, individual and other people's human potential expansion. These will draw out your inner mind power in ways you don't know.

You must know what you want, because clarity (of decision and desire) is your real power. Your conscious mind makes the decision, and your subconscious makes the provision. Christ said, "Pray as though the thing for which you are praying has been received and you shall have it." All of our universe is in service to your mental impression of whatever it is you really want. You are where you are now because that's where you wanted to be.

Allow your imagination the freedom to want anything that you'd like, no matter how seemingly outrageous. Assume for the moment that you have a magic wand or a wish-fulfilling genie that will make your desire reality. You cannot fail. You have all the possible resources (money, time, personnel, et. al.) you could request at your beck and call. The question is, "*What do you want?*" What are your most outrageous, far-out, seemingly impossible tasks?

Let's consider a few examples worthy of noting:

Dr. Robert Schuller, previously mentioned, has a television ministry, which increased his church attendance dramatically, until his walk-in, drive-in, church was literally bursting at the seams. (This is what David, the Psalmist, promised, was the destiny of every thinking, spiritually-oriented worker when he said, "My cup runneth over." Dr. Schuller wanted a church where you could see the beautiful blue sky as he preached in Southern California. He had an outrageous dream of 4,000 seats. The initial cost for his church project was estimated at six million dollars. He had previously raised a million for his Tower of Hope. He had an excellent track record, and he needed a gigantic dream to fire his own and his congregation's growth and development. Previously he had hit on the idea of writing out *Ten Outrageous Solutions* to any problem. His problem was how to obtain six million dollars. He brain-trusted these ten ideas.[1] He says in his tape series called "The Peek-To-Peak Principle":

---

[1] Because of earthquake building codes, the building costs ultimately exceeded $20 million.

44

1) Find one person to give six million dollars. (The church has since been given land valued at more than this amount by John Crean, chairman of the board of Fleetwood Enterprises in Riverside, California. 2) Find six people to give one million dollars each. (Over eight people, such as Clem Stone, Rich DeVos, Frank Sinatra, John Wayne, and several anonymous donors, gave a million.) A lesson to be learned here is that we are admonished by Christ to "Ask and ye shall receive." Most of us forget that we can be like children and ask, ask, ask. We can get whatever we want in business and life. 3) Collect one million dollars at a Sunday service. (This was unheard of; Schuller's imagination created it.) 4) Find twelve people to give five hundred thousand dollars each. 5) Sell ten thousand memorial windows at five hundred dollars each. (This sold out immediately.) 6) Sell ten thousand hanging stars at five hundred dollars each. (This was also an immediate success.) 7) Hold a Beverly Sills Benefit Concert in the 3,000 seat Crystal Cathedral at fifteen hundred dollars each. He says, "Nobody has a money problem; its only an idea problem."

The pygmalion effect in psychology states that you get what you expect to get — if you expect little, you get little; if you expect a lot, you get a lot. I get thousands of letters stating that those who actively employ this principle are now earning more per month than they ever expected to earn annually. W. Clement Stone, founder and Chief Executive Officer of Combined Insurance Companies, headquartered in Chicago, says to his salespeople, "Your goal should be to earn as much per month as most people do per year, then as much per week as most people do per year, then as much per hour, etc." He earns as much per second as most people do in a lifetime. And he is a great, philanthropic steward of his billions of dollars of resources. He and his wife, Jessie Stone, annually contribute hundreds of millions of dollars, not to mention their ideas, time, effort, reputation, experience, and inspiration. I encourage you to read any of this great man's many inspirational books, then listen to his tapes, and if possible, hear him speak in person. Write his Chicago offices for his speaking schedule. He will totally motivate you.

You now have the tools to think outrageous thoughts and then discover the solution to them. Please do it now and write me as you accomplish them and tell me of your exciting unfoldment.

You have 18 billion brain cells
waiting to be activated
by a big goal.

CHAPTER 6

GOAL PREPARATION

I was scuba-diving under ninety feet of beautiful, clear, emerald green water off the island of Martinique when I discovered that I had not checked out the tank I was wearing before I dove. To my chagrin, dismay, anguish, and horror, I noted that I was swimming on my reserve tank, and there was no oxygen left. I gasped, and there was nothing there to inhale. I signaled my diving partner, but he thought I was goofing around because we had been in the water such a short time. Without available air, I panicked and surged for the surface. My panic caught his attention, and he rushed to my aid, complete with his diving skills and wisdom. As I was racing to the top, I was ignorantly holding my breath. This would have caused my lungs to explode. As a skillful diver, he caught me and attempted to reduce my ascending speed and to calm me. This was futile because my adrenalin was pumping, my eyes were fixed on the breaking surface. As an adept diver, he started hitting me in my stomach so I would release some air. This procedure was only partially effective. In total experienced wisdom, he jammed his fingers into my mouth, and I started exhaling like champagne bubbles. It was glorious to release the air and get back my life. He saved my life, and I am thankful for that emergency wisdom. I still love diving, thanks to him. Only now I am more prepared.

Likewise, goal preparation will save you much pain, hurt, and anguish. Set big goals and then break them down into "do-able" daily parts. The cliche that "anything is a cinch inch-by-inch, by yard, it's hard" is essentially true. To be a millionaire, start by earning a dollar, then ten, then one hundred, then one thousand, then ten thousand, then one hundred thousand, then one million. J. Willard Marriott, who founded the international corporation involved in lodging, food service, and the entertainment business, said that when he came to Washington, D.C. in 1927, he owed two thousand dollars. Now he owes twenty million dollars, and that's progress. Not bad for a corporation that had two billion dollars in sales in 1981, and is doubling its total facilities in 1985.

I've witnessed super-star salespeople whose belief systems temporarily outdistance their immediate capabilities (and have watched their self-defeating and escapist reactions). I say "temporarily" because if your goal penetrates and permeates the inner spaces of your mind as a crystal clear visualization of your imagination, it will inevitably become your realization. Dr. Kenneth McFarland has frequently said, "Spectacular success in life is always and only preceded by unspectacular preparation."

You are always demonstrating who you are. As Emerson said, "Who you are speaks so loudly, I can't hear what you are saying." You are forever demonstrating what you really feel and think.

Be happy with all your demonstrations, whether they are positive or negative. As your awareness about

49

yourself and your true capabilities are field tested you will be able to make even better demonstrations. Children learn to crawl, walk, run, and bicycle. They want to drive cars, fly planes, and take shuttles to intergalactic destinations. Those are all demonstrations that start in thought and become reality through practice and experience.

Goals are new forward-moving objectives. They magnetize you toward them. However, they are currently outside your comfort zone, or you would have obtained them already.

New goals attract you. However, other people will occasionally ridicule, reject, and refute your goals. Expect it, and don't let them stop you. I specialize in showing you how to overcome negativism — yours and others — to go on to new horizons.

Life is a marathon, not a sprint. It's important to know that. Some commercials ignorantly intimate that life is a sprint and one can "instantly" have a dazzling self-image, perfect aroma, brighter teeth, sex-appeal, abundant friendship, travel, or whatever is being merchandised. Such commercialism promotes unrealistic expectations, beliefs, and opinions. Life is not instant. Life is a long trek with plenty of adventures, detours, asides, and surprises. If it were otherwise, it would be bland, dull, and monotonous.

Dr. George Sheehan, cardiologist, runner, and philosophical writer par excellence, says, "If you finish a marathon (26 miles, 385 yards), you win." Likewise, the mere act of writing down *too many goals* (your marathon)

establishes the connection with their unfolding achievement, and you *win*. Congratulations!

Describing your desires
on these pages
is the initial step
to the physical
realization.

CHAPTER 7

THE LAW OF ASSUMPTION

The Law of Assumption states that you consciously assume that your desires will be fulfilled. The principle is simple but not easy. Your ideas create your reality. To really assume an idea, you must dwell on it with a relentless fixity of thought. The new conception (assumption) must permeate and penetrate the inner spaces of your mind prior to out-picturing it. Holding fast to a concept and repeating it faithfully will ultimately bring it into existence.

Brian Epstein and the Beatles intrinsically used the Law of Assumption to revolutionize music in the Sixties. Independently, each Beatle, John (while alive), Paul, George, and Ringo have never gotten caught up in facts but have forever used the Law of Assumption and imagination into reality — new music, new haircuts, new customs, new clothes, new films, new life-styles, and new thinking. The beauty of the Law of Assumption is that if an idea will work for anyone, you can assume it will work for you. The movie, "Jazz Singer," with Neil Diamond, epitomizes this principle.

This principle is boundless. It released Bill Sands legally from prison, when Warden Clinton Duffy inspired him to read *Think and Grow Rich*, literally and between the lines. He got the message. That's why it's important to read success, self-help action, and metaphysical books to stay inspired to the Law of Assumption. It's obvious by results that Johnny Carson believes and assumes that he has endless staying and paying power on the "Tonight Show." He has outlasted all talk-show contenders.

My own **Future Diary** activities prove daily that the Law of Assumption rests easily on having clear desires, written in detail. It's fascinating and true that the more you employ this great principle, the better and faster it works. Alan Alda, TV star of "M.A.S.H.," aggressively assumes his expanding abilities as an actor, a movie star, director, and producer. The only limit is your belief system. However, please use it repetitively in small ways so that you establish self-confidence. The ultimate user of this principle was Jesus Christ. His word was immediate law and realization. Best of all, the Master said, "Go thou and do likewise." Translated into modern colloquialism, that means, "You can do it."

The great news is that, should every living human learn and actively employ this phenomenal principle, it could not wear out, rust, tarnish, or get tired. It's eternal, like the principle $2 \times 2 = 4$. It will be so no matter how frequently used.

Continue reading and re-reading this Law of Assumption until you have ownership of the idea. You will know the principle is yours from the repetitive, successful results you start generating. You will eventually demonstrate good in everything you do. Incidentally, please note that the Infinite has manufactured enough good for everyone. This is because the resources of the Infinite are infinite.

The Law of Assumption requires that your feeling nature totally identifies with your desire. Have a deep conviction that you've fulfilled your mission and that all is well. All conceptions and assumptions that are felt and fixed in mind will be embodied in the world. Nancy Reagan says, "(President) Ronald Reagan never really wanted anything like he wanted our 688 acre ranch in the Santa Ynez Mountains (by Santa Barbara, California)." He wanted it, and he got it. Each of us, whether a pauper or the President of the United States gets what we assume we can have.

It's not that people
want too much,
it's that they want
too little.

I WANT TO HAVE

Begin by listing three tangible goals and three intangible goals.

Thinking is what life
is all about.
The most important thing
you can think about
is your life.

I WANT TO DO

Write down your hopes, plans, aspirations, and high purposes.

Dreams are the
touchstones
of our characters.

Henry David Thoreau (1817 - 1862)

SELECT ANOTHER GOAL
TO MATERIALIZE
IN YOUR MIND'S EYE.

Change your thoughts
and you
change your world.

CHAPTER 8

EVALUATE YOUR GOALS

By the end of three years of active goal-writing and accomplishment, you will be a professional goal-setting, goal-getter who will: 1) understand totally the principle, procedure, and process of goal visualization, verbalization, and realization; 2) have studied yourself and others in depth; 3) understand that goal-setting is causal and gets results; and 4) have developed a lifetime habit of goal-setting, study, and accomplishment that will enrich your life, your family, and your world.

I assume that you regularly attend motivational, educational, and inspirational seminars; this, of course, should be continued and supported by active cassette tape listening.

You have a legitimate right to ask, "What will goal-planning do for me?" It will do as much as you can conceive and believe. Joe Gandolfo used it to become the world's number one life insurance salesman by selling 1.1 billion dollar's worth of life insurance in one year. The discipline of goal-planning can literally take you from wherever you are to wherever you want to be. The question is, "Where do you want to be?"

You are where you are now because, in your heart, that's where you want to be. Change the desires of your heart and head, and you'll automatically start changing your results. You can be almost anything, do almost anything, go almost everywhere. You must simply write your goals down.

No one wants to be a weakling, yet non-goal directed individuals are weak; their destination is foggy and vague. Clarity of goals, backed by decisive action, is power. The way to grow strong is to associate with other goal-directed super-achievers. They want your friendship as you want theirs.

Whether you feel that you are ready or not, begin at once to set goals. There's no excuse not to. It's an erroneous belief to "cop out" and say such things as "I am too old, too young, too tall, too short, too smart, too dumb, too busy, too lazy, too ignorant." Or worse yet, "I'll remember them," as we are all instant forgetters.

Not setting goals (or wanting to set goals) is an expression of a negative mental attitude and low self-esteem. The greatest problem is that negative minded individuals rationalize their difficulty. The current jargon is, "I'll go with the flow," "Whatever will be will be," and "I live for today only."

Satisfaction and fulfillment are a by-product of moving in the direction of your heart's desire. Goals make life meaningful, interesting, vital, and exciting. Humans are problem-solving, problem-having animals that need objectives. God invented your mind as a teleological instrument that sets and gets goals. Goals focus our attention, and where the attention goes the energy flows. We each need a regular, daily sense of accomplishment — of having moved forward. With this our self-esteem grows, blooms, and develops; without it, our self-esteem withers and dies.

During our youth we learned life's rules and limitations, all the "don'ts", all the "dos", all the "shoulds" and all the "have-tos." Re-think them now in light of goal-setting and choose what you will believe.

Whatever limiting belief you have allowed to slow you down, to stifle or to stop you: eradicate it! No one limits you except your own thoughts, feelings, beliefs, and attitudes. *Go for greatness.*

One of the times Christ became upset is when the man buried his talent. The Master said, "Oh, you wicked and slothful servant." I understand that concept to mean that you and I are supposed to maximize our talents, assets, and abilities. Attempt great things. Other people will come to support, encourage. admire, appreciate, and respect your courageous convictions and boldness.

We are
what we think about.

MENTAL GOALS

Give yourself time limitations that see you to these achievements. Then set new ones.

> *books I will read*
> *audio-tapes I will hear*
> *music I will listen to*
> *speakers I will experience*
> *courses I will take*

My interest is in the future
because I am going to spend
the rest of my life there.
Charles F. Kettering (1876 - 1958)

HEALTH GOALS

my desired weight
my desired measurements
my daily exercise program
my diet
my sleep regimen
playtime

He who asks of life nothing but
the improvement of his own nature...
is less liable than anyone else
to miss and waste life.

Henri Frederic Amiel (1821 - 1881)

EMOTIONAL GOALS

to accept my feelings
to develop courage
to offer understanding to others

If a man takes no thought
about what is distant,
he will find sorrow near at hand.
Confucius (c. 551 - 479 B.C.)

FINANCIAL GOALS

Quantify goals in these areas and set a schedule for accomplishing them.

income

savings

investments

tithing

projects

There is only one success —
to be able to spend your life
in your own way.

Christopher Morley (1870 - 1957)

CAREER GOALS

Qualify these goals and set a schedule for accomplishing them.

becoming more effective

developing contacts

securing a promotion

Time goes, you say?
Ah no,
alas, time stays,
we go.

Austin Dobson (1840 - 1921)

FAMILY GOALS

Schedule time to spend with your family. Make this priority time.

> *house chores*
> *leisure activities*
> *shared time with mate*
> *shared time with children*
> *shared time with parents*

Every man is worth
just so much
as the things are worth
about which he busies himself.

Marcus Aurelius (A.D. 121 -180)

SOCIAL GOALS

people to meet
people to get to know
keeping in touch
entertaining

Life is a series of collisions with the future;
it is not the sum of what we have been
but what we yearn to be.

Jose Ortega y Gasset (1883 - 1955)

VICTORIES & ACCOMPLISHMENTS

Write down your goals as if they have already been accomplished, giving dates.

> *In 1990, I inspired an audience of 10,000*
> *In 1992, I bought a red Rolls Royce.*

Every thought
in the subconscious is created;
ultimately it demonstrates itself.

SPIRITUAL GOALS

prayer
meditation
church attendance
believing in myself

The only waste
of human resources
is to let them go unused.

LOVE OF GIVING

Consider: What have I to give out of the love of selfless giving.

to myself
to my family
to my work
to my church
to my community
to the world

A man who dares
to waste one hour of time
has not discovered
the value of life.
Charles Darwin (1809 - 1882)

MY LOVES

Write the names of the people you love. Include mentors, people with tremendous capabilities and knowledge which they are willing to share — people you would like to imitate, emulate, match, and surpass.

Reflect . . .
grow . . .
plan . . .
enjoy . . .
experience
a life renaissance.

I AM THANKFUL

Let this list grow day by day.
four things I am thankful for today.

May you live all the days
of your life.

Jonathan Swift (1667 - 1745)

EACH DAY ADD FOUR MORE THINGS YOU ARE
THANKFUL FOR.

CHAPTER 9

AWAKEN A HIDDEN GENIUS

Is goal-setting really worth the investment of time, energy, and effort? You bet it is!

Your subconscious probably helped you to master the art of riding a bicycle. Now, even if you haven't been on a bicycle in ten years, assuming you are still physically able, your subconscious has an automatic pilot that will facilitate your getting on a bicycle and peddling easily and effortlessly away. Likewise, some small amount of effort is required to become a disciplined goal-setter; over time, this artform will pay you back unbelievable dividends and undeclared benefits that are now virtually impossible for you to conceive and believe. I say this because it has been true of every goal-setter in history, including Henry Ford, who conceived mass-production and mass-distribution as a principle and saw it realized; Conrad Hilton, who built his worldwide namesake hotel chain; and Thomas Edison, who said, "I'll be the world's greatest inventor." Edison's subconscious tapping of infinite intelligence (which resides within us all) realized 1,097 major inventions, only four of which we don't actively use today.

Goals overcome weakness, fear, and sickness. For health reasons, my friend, Cavett Robert, and his wife and five children had to leave a law practice in New York and move to Phoenix, Arizona at a young age. Six doctors told him he might live for six months. Not able to immediately practice law, he set out to sell homes and insurance and did a phenomenal job. Overcome with the activity of self-insuring his family's future welfare, in a six-month period he became the top realty and insurance salesman in America's Southwest, acquired financial independence, and overcame his disease. Busy, accomplishment-oriented people don't have time to be ill. Robert now jokes that he outlived the six doctors who willingly predicted his early demise and states, "Those six months have been the best 48 years of my life."

What are your goals? What quests and challenges are you giving to your mind?

Seeing myself as a success,
feeling myself as a success,
believing in my success,
I am success.

I AM

Personalized goals must be stated in the first person: I AM. I Am is your self-definition in process. We instantly and constantly contract with ourselves to become whatever we attach to the words I AM. Write everything good that you are and want to be.

Etch the thought
into the fabric of your being
until you become it.

YOU ARE

Restate your goals in the second person: YOU ARE.

Add to the list.

> *You are a happy person.*
>
> *You are a loyal and true friend.*
>
> *You are a terrific thinker.*
>
> *You are responsible for your life.*

Your future emanates
totally and absolutely
from your present
mental attitude.

_____ IS

Restate your goals in the third person, using your full name.

Repeat them aloud early in the morning and late at night.

Reiterate twice daily for one month.

Man is what he believes.

Anton Chekov (1860 - 1904)

CHAPTER 10

MIND SOLUTION

The more masterful you get at writing down goals and obtaining them, the faster they appear. You will reach that state of consciousness wherein what you think about comes about (demonstrates itself) almost immediately. Let me give you a perfect example. I love to be well dressed at all times and in all places. While working I wear tailor-made shirts, and though they are perfectly fitted, dry cleaners often ignorantly or carelessly press my collar stays into my collars, making them limp and less than maximally attractive. My wife Patty and I started pulling them out of my collars prior to dropping them off at the laundry; however, some were still heat-stamped in. I had a vision that there must be a solution to that problem. I let my mind rest in the answer.

Overnight, Patty said, "I've got a special gift for you." Enclosed in a jewelry-type foldable velvet pouch were 14 K gold plated, four-inch-long collar stays. Ta Da! Exactly what I wanted. I can assure you I never forget my stays in my collar anymore. Romans 11:33 says, "His ways are beyond finding out." Put your mind on the solution and not the problem. Be ever ready to recognize the solution when it appears, as it will, if and when you are ready.

CHAPTER 11

GOAL SETTING IS FREE!

It doesn't cost a cent to set goals. The only one preventing you from setting goals is you. Start now. Begin at once to set and get goals, whether you are ready or not. Doing it will banish your fear of failure and your fear of success. You will be amazed, intrigued and delighted at the positive results. W. Clement Stone says, "If you have everything to gain and nothing to lose by trying, by all means try."

Total freedom is available in diary-writing because your thoughts are for your eyes only. It's private in nature, unless you choose to share it. I've found that the first act of being willing to start writing down goals is the hardest. Once one recognizes the phenomenal potential benefits and starts his pen or pencil going, jotting down his desires, watch out! His or her imagination tingles as it is titillated with the excitement that just maybe it's possible to acquire a Mercedes 450 SL, a Rolex watch, fourteen dresses, a fur coat, three national or international vacations a year, friendships with famous people, deepening love, personal growth and financial freedom — just by putting a few drops of ink on paper. It seems incredible and unbelievable but the testimonials are real, honest, and truthful. And besides, if it will work for others — why not you? Start now as a Future Diarist, begin whether you are ready or not. Poise your pen and start writing out all your most intimate, tangible, and intangible heart's desire.

You will meet the real you as you write in your diary, and that's important. You will discover what you really think and how your consciousness evolves over time. Save old diaries, as they will be a recurring source of joy and pleasure as you review your mountains of past accomplishments and look continually to future challenges. The beauty of your mind will reflect and radiate back to you as your ideas take form.

When Piggly Wiggly's founder, Clarence Saunders, opened his first store, everyone laughed at his creative new self-service shopping cart idea. To think that someone wanted to wait on him or herself and would roll a cart around a prearranged grocery store was ridiculous to traditional grocers. They stopped laughing when everyone began buying more and faster at Piggly Wiggly. Sales in the first six months increased 300 percent because of convenience, while saving on store clerks and losses on credit sales.

Saunders was a poorly educated Virginian who grew up in Tennessee working in lumber mills and tobacco sheds, eventually graduating into the grocery business. In 1916 he invented a wicker basket on wheels to make shopping easy and effortless. One man with one goal of automating grocery stores made a vast change in the food-shopping habits of countless millions. What can you do with your goal?

When you know clearly
what you want
you'll get it with
accelerating acceleration.

WRITE A MINUTELY DETAILED DESCRIPTION OF YOUR PRIMARY GOAL.

See it in your mind's eye as if it is already yours.
Can you visualize it? Can you feel it?

CHAPTER 12

SUPPLY IS INFINITE

Since Thomas Malthus, the economist, in 1797, said, "There is not enough food to go around," individuals have believed in fundamental scarcity. The truth of the universe is that there is now, always has been, and will always be a supply in the universe. This endless supply is hidden from individual understanding only by lack of inner awareness of the truth. God pours an unfailing supply daily onto this spaceship called Earth to feed over five billion human inhabitants, as well as the countless trillions of forms of life from His inexhaustible *resources*. Inside your mind you must feel and believe in the fundamental abundance of your world. God is the *giver*, who has never known lack or limitation and doesn't want you to either. Learn to think exclusively in terms of abundant supply. Apply this principle to millions of particular personal experiences.

The true world of *causation* lies within your mind. What you experience in life, whether prosperity or poverty, is the *effect* of your thoughts. Change your thinking (goals), and you automatically change your results. To change your world from good to phenomenally good, change your thinking — not the conditions, situations, and circumstances of your life. You out-picture in your experience the goals you have meditatively been in-picturing in your mind's eye.

When you write down your goals, you are at cause and you bring yourself to a point in consciousness where they are realized already — all you do is catch up to them. Supply is constant — it is infinite. It can be tapped equally by all who are positively and correctly using their minds. What are the channels through which the results occur? The temporary channels of supply are many and varied. Supply for you has come through your mother, father, odd jobs, steady jobs, free-lancing, sundry insurances, pensions, inheritances, and businesses. Channels are inherently temporary; therefore, do not fix your attention on channels but rather the source which is in your *mind*.

Individuals erroneously believe that the company for which they work is their channel of supply. The never-ceasing supply is really God (good) coming through your mind. The resources of the Infinite are infinite, so set your goals with regard only to how much you can accept, enjoy, use, share, and contribute to others. Your increasing demands create more supply. Be open to the resources of the Infinite.

Affirmation:
The words you say to yourself
or others say to you
that you think about
and act upon
and that ultimately
act upon you.

GIVE YOURSELF POSITIVE AFFIRMATIONS.

I am a happy person
I am a loyal and true friend
I am a nurturing parent
I am an inspired artist
I am a dynamic executive

The world's conditioning
is so complete
that we must spend half our lives
unlearning what we have learned,
reprogramming ourselves
for what we want to know.

We are influenced by what we hear others say about us —
"YOU ARE." Nine out of ten of these inputs are denials
or negatives. You are erasing them now.

Give yourself more positive affirmations beginning with
YOU ARE.

Principle:
Ideas are always created
as forms.

ADD TO THIS LIST EVERY DAY.
REACH FOR THE SKY!

CHAPTER 13

MONEY

Money is a yardstick measuring the services you have rendered. The higher the quantity and quality of service rendered — honestly and ethically — with a positive mental attitude, the greater the compensation. Compensation is almost always directly proportionate to your effort, the vehicle used for earning, your self-imaging, your desire and your established goals. Money is a psychic vibration. It comes to those who affirm: "I am rich, prosperous and abundant." This happens because the mind is deductive and goes from general to specific. Whatever your subconscious mind deducts, it will produce. As you want more you may change your channel (occupation) of acceptance. For example, a public school teacher, no matter how high quality, has some limitations as the system is currently established. However, with intensified desire for wealth and opulence, let's say that individual applies his/her skill in a direct sales occupation with unlimited opportunity and potential. I have witnessed thousands of such individuals leapfrog financially forward from earning roughly $20,000 annually to in excess of $250,000 annually. The difference is one of vehicle. Your obligation in whatever you are doing is to do it well and do it with excellence. You are directly and indirectly affecting everyone else. Assuming you are in a highly profitable business, I believe you are obligated to earn surplus wealth to create more jobs for the less talented, be a great financial steward, promote worthy causes, and be a philanthropist helping others to help themselves — give a hand-up not a handout. Handouts, as you know, rip off people's self-esteem and self-worth. One of your goals may, wisely be, to earn as much as you can, save as much as you can, invest as much as you can, and give as much as you can.

And in today already walks tomorrow.
Samuel Taylor Coleridge (1772 - 1834)

ECONOMIC WANTS

Consider your economic wants:

whole life
next ten years
next five years
this year
this week
today

Time is a priority.
We all invest it wisely
when we are on purpose
when we are dedicated
to the business
of accomplishing our lives.

CHAPTER 14

BIG GOALS

Big goals stimulate and motivate you to get moving and keep moving.

When writing, forget all the requirements and restrictions you learned in school. Do your own thing. It's your diary, written for you, by you. Free yourself of conventions and rules. If pictures are impressed upon your mind, let your pen put them to paper. Forget about misspellings, grammar, punctuation, etc. Write to you about you. Feel encouraged to brag, praise, dream big, pray, love, and write poetry, as the inspiration hits. Often you will look back at your impressions and be impressed as you release your imprisoned splendor. Allow for flow, spontaneity, and intuition to express themselves.

You can even ask yourself progressively bigger questions, and your mind will ultimately and immediately answer them. My intellectual mentor, Dr. R. Buckminster Fuller, was forever asking himself bigger questions, like: "What is universe?" and requiring himself to answer based on his own experience. You do the same. There is genius potential inside your mind awaiting release by writing it down. Bucky, as he was affectionately called, was considered the Leonardo Da Vinci of our time because he used the "write it down" principle, as did Da Vinci. I am not trying to tell you about this phenomenally powerful idea. I am trying to sell you on it, so you will use it and forever keep harvesting better results. Dr. Fuller said, "Great ideas emerge from the metaphysical mustiness."

Never fear looking at blank pages of your **Future Diary** and my thought stimulators. I hope these thought stimulators will launch you into thinking you own thoughts.

Occasionally, to stimulate even more of your mind/brain resources, write through the perception of one of your mentors or heroes. Put your mind in theirs and ask yourself if you were he/she, what would you think, do, or say. To go the extra mile with this idea, as actors and actresses do, attempt to live the role and jot down your reflections.

Mehdi Fakhazedhi, a Persian born to great wealth, was educated as an attorney in Iran. He wanted to get a Ph.D. in the American University system and flew to the United States without knowing a bit of English. Upon arrival, he wanted to go to Salt Lake City. He was told to travel by bus. For three days and three nights he ventured painfully forth. Upon arrival there he met a friend who told him that he must learn English in high school prior to entry into the university. He did. While doing his graduate studies, he fell in love with a beautiful lady from Ireland. He pursued her with all his heart, mind, and spirit — even changing schools to be near her. Against her will, her parents' will, his parents' will, and his friends' will, he finally wowed and wed her. Without any prior planning and when he was within hours of his doctoral graduation, she became pregnant. He rushed out to get a job, asking his school counselor for employment in international export and banking. The counselor suggested insurance as a third choice. He went for an interview at Metropolitan Life Insurance Company. The interviewer asked, "Do you own any insurance?" His answer was "No." Mehdi explained his situation and respectfully requested that he be given a chance to study and take the test. He was and passed. He was given a debit (an area where the sales agent makes weekly house calls to collect pennies). It was a humiliating indignity for Mehdi to collect money on 47th Street in New York, an area called "Hell's Kitchen." His heart was broken, and he wanted to quit, but his philosophy was, "Nothing is impossible!" So he decided to succeed first and then quit. Succeed he did. He sucked it in and toughed it out. He became Metropolitan's number one life insurance agent. He annually sells millions of dollars' worth of life insurance. His eye is fixed on personally producing five hundred million dollars' worth of business in one year, and then he will call himself a success. He is totally amazing. He is one of the highest quality human beings that I have ever met. I totally encourage you to hear him speak. Also, read his biography, *Nothing is Impossible*, by Roy Alexander. It will raise you out of your indifference and procrastination and move you to think big and achieve big.

One of the biggest and most remarkable achievers of all times is Dr. Armand Hammer, M.D. At age nineteen, he was graduating from Columbia Medical, when his father's pharmaceutical business started to falter and have problems. Young Armand thoughtfully discovered that tincture of ginger was selling, briskly, so he proceeded to corner the market and make a million dollars, virtually overnight, by smart thinking and smart action. Upon graduation he decided to go to Russia with a medical wagon and help out the hurting peasantry. Once there he personally witnessed painful starvation. He met Lenin and said he would invest one million dollars into wheat and food stuffs for import trade agreements and privileges in the U.S.S.R. He got it; in fact, Lenin said, "We need businessmen here, not medical doctors." Eventually, Dr. Hammer got thirty-eight major importing licenses, including one from Henry Ford. Henry Ford understood Hammer's belief that international commerce is the best way to world peace. When Stalin entered the scene, Hammer was immediately evicted. Hammer asked for and got some of the great Czarist art treasures, which he commercialized in the States, making yet another fortune.

Eventually, after prospering greatly in several ventures (cattle, alcohol, art), he planned to retire permanently to California. His C.P.A. suggested, for tax purposes, that he invest in a penny stock company with three employees, called Occidental Petroleum. He bought 51 percent and hired the best earth geologist to look for oil. The rest is history. Hammer became inspired, set big-big goals, took over as chairman of the board, and Occidental has become the twelfth largest company in the world, employing over 50,000 people. Recently, Occidental bought City Services, making it the world's fifth largest company.

Mary Kay Ash, chairperson of the board and founder of Mary Kay Cosmetics, started her company at retirement time after having written down a formula for an ideal sales company. She liked the notion so much that she gave birth to her dream with an investment of five thousand dollars. Her company has bloomed and prospered throughout the United States, Canada, Argentina, and is, according to her son Richard Rogers, corporate president, going to become the number one skin care company in America by 1990. Today they are the sixth biggest skin care company in the U.S. and moving forward fast with over 150,000 consultants. Many of their national directors are earning total commissions and overrides of over five hundred thousand dollars per year and expecting that to become over one million dollars per year. It is amazing what an inspired idea can do for the originator and all the fellow perpetrators. If you've never been to an exciting direct sales meeting, I encourage you to attend a Mary Kay Regional Rally or call about attending an Amway, NeoLife, Shaklee seminar or convention. The excitement generated at such a gathering will help you raise your aim, ambition, and achievement enormously. There's greatness inside each one of us wanting and waiting to be tapped. Submit yourself to the catalytic stimulus.

The question is, "What can one person do?" One person ecstatic about a goal can do anything.

We can do all things
if we will.

Leon Battista Alberti (1404 - 1472)

MY SPIRITUAL WANTS

Consider your spiritual wants:
whole life
next ten years
next five years
this year
this week
today

CHAPTER 15

POWERFULLY FOCUSED

Goal-setting works best when it includes someone else. My wife and I establish meaningful goals together. Often times my mind races with ideas, of which, maybe only one in a hundred is totally useful. We are so close that she gently tells me that attempting this or that is an operation in futility. What this means is that an important other person can keep you powerfully focused, keep you on track toward your top priority and objectives, and encourage you repetitively to these accomplishments.

Victor Frankl's (psychiatrist - author) goal while incarcerated in a German prison camp, was to hold his wife's hand again, look into her eyes again, and write a manuscript, which later became an outstanding book – *Man's Search for Meaning.* Dr. Frankl's observation during imprisonment was that people with a goal in life survived war and its humiliations, emotional and nutritional starvation, et. al. They had a definitive goal in life to live and so do you.

Animals have intrinsic goals, i.e., you can almost set your clock by the buzzard's animal migratory return to Hinkley, Ohio; the swallows to San Juan Capistrano; and the monarch butterflies to Ventura, California and other areas.

In your goal-setting establish a self-rewarding system of pay-offs, even for little achievements. Then set the goal and mentally dwell only on the rewards of its achievement.

When I was nine years old, my parents took my brothers and me to Denmark. My father's objective was to teach us Danish by the immersion method. Prior to "super learning techniques," it was the best way to learn a language.

Additionally, I became addicted to low-handle-bar racing bicycles. This was before they became vogue in the United States. I wanted one with my whole heart. I asked my father if I could have one, and he said, "Yes, when you are 21 years old." I persisted, "You don't understand. I want it now!"

After much discussion, my subconscious intuitively figured out "how" to get the bicycle. My father had taught my brothers and me that "free enterprise means, 'the more enterprising you are, the more free you are.'" Given that belief, I said, "Dad, can I have it if I earn it myself?" He said, "Yes," assuming I'd never earn $175 in six months' time. (That's the equivalent in inflated dollars today of $675.) I already had a paper route and was earning thirty-seven cents a day, enough to buy a bicycle magazine from England, from which I cut out a colored picture of the exact bicycle I wanted and hung it on the wall next to my bed. It said, "Ride a wheel on Sheffield Steele $175." I could visualize myself enjoying that bicycle and winning races.

While working to earn the bicycle, I saw an advertisement in my Boy Scout Magazine that said I could sell greeting cards on consignment. I said to myself, "I can afford that." I sent for the Christmas cards and zealously went out to sell them, keeping in my mind's eye, the bicycle I wanted to earn. In the brevity of one month, I sold 376 boxes of Christmas cards. Did I want to sell Christmas cards? "No!" Did I want to be the number one greeting card salesman in the nine-year-old division? "No!" What did I want?; The bicycle! What did I get? The bicycle and the bonus of embryonic sales skills that would serve me for the rest of my life. This is the kind of result you can achieve by staying focused on your desires.

We have no greater
or lesser conquest
than over ourselves.

Leonardo da Vinci (1452 - 1519)

PERSONAL GROWTH

There is no growth in life without the development of one's own unique self. Write:

how I want to grow
mentally
physically
emotionally
spiritually

You ought to be afraid to die
until you've contributed
something great
back to humanity.

Oliver Wendell Holmes (1809 - 1894)

CHAPTER 16

IMAGINARY CONVERSATIONS

You can even do imaginative things like participate in imaginary conversations and dialogues with persons living or dead, partaking of their wisdom and insights by invoking their vibratory presence. For a more complete explanation of this outrageous idea, read Napoleon Hill's *Think and Grow Rich*, about his nightly discussions with Emerson, Lincoln, Burbank, etc. In his controlled state of mental reverie these personalities came alive and chatted with him about whatever he wanted to discuss. I have interviewed a billionaire who uses this principle regularly to solve his knottiest problems.

Future is creative stuff
that can be constructed
as we like it.
It only requires
predawn blueprints
so that you can make your way
smooth, beautiful, and perfect.

CHAPTER 17

SELF-PORTRAIT

For extra fun, write out a self-portrait. Write your own biography as it is and as you would like it to be. Read other people's biographies and autobiographies for inspiration. As an embryonic speaker I literally poured over hundreds of other speaker's biographies, distilling in my mind's eye the qualities, values, virtues and accomplishments that I am still aggregating into my biography. It's fun to detail out your progressive biography. Do it now! The true you is faceless, formless spirit that receives identity when you say, "I am *this* or *that*." Therefore, write your own self-portrait.

Destiny is not a matter of chance,
it is a matter of choice;
it is not a thing to be waited for,
it is a thing to be achieved.

William Jennings Bryan (1860 - 1925)

CHAPTER 18

THE DREAM GOALS GAME

The dream goals game is played with two or more cooperative participants. Perhaps the members are relatives, friends, colleagues, associates, mentor-mentee, or some such relationship that provides workable harmony and periodic frequency of contact.

It works this way: At each regular meeting (weekly at best) one individual states his or her dream. The others are allowed to question the dream and see if it is really true, vital, important, and meaningful to that individual. Assuming it is a deeply held desire, and the others agree it's viable/attainable, then they cooperate to commit to realize it as expeditiously as possible.

My friend, Sam Curtis, was a businessman par excellence and spokesman-promoter of a concept called "Family Time," where family members invest meaningful time together. He taught me this phenomenal concept called "The Dream Goal Game." He took it into his family of twelve children and said, "when I am home (he traveled extensively as chairman of a six hundred million dollar corporation), we will be together as a family from dinner until 9:00 p.m. each evening, and your friends are welcome. Each night one of us gets to share our dream."

At one family get-together, his son Scott said, "I want to be a *winner* like the rest of the Curtis clan." (This family teaches and practices intense family love, respect, pride, loyalty and fraternity. They feel they have the "greatest family in the world.") Scott was born blind. After several operations, his vision is still upside down and backwards, so he has learning difficulties. He has a lot of other talents, such as a high degree of love, perception, and understanding. He wanted to excel academically in junior high school and be on the honor roll just once to show he was part of the great Curtis team. That was his dream.

His sisters volunteered to tutor him academically, reading his assignments to him and even writing down his assignments as needed. Each family member pitched in to help Scott.

At graduation, it was announced that the faculty decided the "Student of the Year" would not be based on the three years a student has gone through school but the last year. The principal at commencement said, "I would like to announce that 'The Student of the Year' is Scott Curtis, who for one full year got perfect scores on everything he did. He saw horizons and expanded his potential, standing higher than anyone has ever stood. And his family stood with him."

You too can play the dream game. Have a big, worth-while cause, and I will guarantee you phenomenal applause!

CHAPTER 19

FIVE MORE TECHNIQUES

There are five vital techniques to writing in your diary:

Lists

Maps of consciousness

Altered point of view

Unsent letter

Dialogues

Each technique is herein covered and explored. Try them all. There is no right way to do your diary.

Lists are time-savers and time-condensors. Business people often have to do lists, "Write memo to Charlie, lunch with Sally, get theatre tickets, etc."

An "Upset" list allows you to vent your resistance, resentments, hurts, and hatreds, i.e., "I hate John's cigar-chomping attitude" or "I haven't got time to write an essay for my final exam."

A list of "Things I am afraid of":

Snakes in springtime

Overacting

The death of a loved one

Possible outbreak of war

Maps of Consciousness use free drawings, intuitive or automatic writing and tap into the inner reserves of your consciousness. See the book *Mind Mapping* for further in-depth explanation.

Altered point of view is getting an objective point of view. I described this in my story about Napoleon Hill's nightly round-table chats with great thinkers.

Unsent letters are your scribblings, usually of deep emotional significance for you, that record your thoughts and feelings and that are always better left unsent. The point is that you release your pent-up emotions so that they don't do you any harm. For a real charge, write a letter to God and then write back God's response to your letter.

Dialogues are a therapeutic technique to have you explore all sides of a situation, condition, relationship, or experience. You can simulate what another will say and anticipate all things. It provides for self-healing and self-guidance. Problems are only stressful if solutions are invisible. This technique can make visible the invisible which, often in retrospect, seems obvious. Experiment with dialogues as a form of great thinking.

FUTURE DIARY
takes you
from the future
to the present.

CHAPTER 20

NOW IT'S UP TO YOU!

Your **Future Diary** is a time machine that will release you from the constrictive limitations of time. It is primarily written by me for you to clarify goals and discover future destinations. However, you can use it to be here now or explore your past. Perhaps you will be sparked to do creative writing that becomes a story, song, or play. Maybe playing in your **Future Diary** will close memory gaps or open up new vistas of information. It will help you to know who you are, what you choose and what you decide. Brilliance and genius often arrive as hunches and thought flashes. Be forever ready to capture your ideas and put them into your **Future Diary**. Be especially ready during the night with pen and paper by your bedside to hook great ideas and pull them in for wakeful use. Red Skelton told me that the angel of inspiration came to him one night with a profound idea which he jotted down. The next morning he awoke to discover, dismayed, that his note said, "write play." He couldn't remember anything about the play. Henceforward, he always carries dictating tape recorders with him to bed, in the bathroom, everywhere. It's his voice actuated **Future Diary**.

Every time you look at your **Future Diary** plan to set more goals; some few will die a natural death, others will flourish, expanding you as a person as they expand.

Be sure to set goals when you feel like it; and when you don't feel like it, set goals until you do feel like it. As an almost daily jogger, I can state unequivocally that occasionally I'd rather not run; however, ten minutes into my routine of running, I am ecstatic, euphoric, and elated that I chose the character building discipline. Don't give your mind lackadaisical suggestions unless you *want* to harvest lackadaisical results. Consistent effort and investment of time and energy pays consistent results. The more wise and prudent people will catch your vision and help you achieve it. The only individual who has to have fixity of vision is you.

Genius is the ability to hold one's own vision steady until it becomes reality. Neville, author of *Resurrection*, which I recommended to readers, says, "Imagination creates reality." I encourage you to modify that and affirm morning, noon, and night, that "My imagination (of these goals) creates my reality (of these goals)." To prove that imagination creates reality, simply read the biographies or autobiographies of Andrew Carnegie, Jay Willard Marriott, Clement Stone, or Helen Keller. Their imaginations were limitless and so is yours once properly activated.

In summation, speak about your goals, primarily to yourself. Tell others only when you feel and believe in advance that they can and will support, benefit, encourage, excite, and help you to move towards your dream.

Remember that your Diary is for your eyes only until you choose to share it. A personal life lived at its fullest is something you can overflow out of after you've done your doing and deservedly want to brag about it.

You control your future, your destiny. What you think about comes about. By recording your dreams and goals on paper, *you* can set in motion the process of becoming the person you most want to be. Put your future in good hands — *your* own.

The more you think about it
the quicker you get it.

SUCCESSES TO COME

Visualize these successes clearly in your mind's eye.

There is no wealth but life.

John Ruskin (1819 - 1900)

Keep adding to these lists, continuously expanding them. Review this diary 20 minutes daily, on rising and retiring. Reach for the sky!

PHOTO CREDITS